A TASTE COOKBOOK

"The Joystick of Cooking"

By Tim Murphy

For information on Tim Murphy's
other "Cookbooks for Guys,"
upcoming releases and merchandise
visit www.flanneljohn.com

A TASTE OF THE 80'S COOKBOOK

"The Joystick of Cooking"

TABLE OF CONTENTS

A VIEW TO A GRILL

1 chicken breast, skinless and boneless
2 tablespoons of mixed herbs, chopped
1 tablespoon of olive oil
1 tablespoon of lemon juice

Mix herbs, oil and juice together thoroughly. Coat the chicken with the mixture and seal up in an aluminum foil packet. Grill over medium-high heat for 12 minutes.

ALL HOT DOGS GO TO HEAVEN

Hot Dogs
(Vienna, David Burg, Hebrew National,
Nathan's and Ballpark brands preferred)
Poppy Seed buns (if available)
Dill pickle spears
Cucumber spears
Tomato slices
Pickled peppers or sport peppers
Diced onion
Mustard (yellow)
Sweet relish (electric green if available)
Celery salt
NO KETCHUP!

Grill or boil the hot dogs. Use very soft, fresh buns or steam them if needed. Load up your dogs with all the ingredients saving the celery salt for first and last.

APPLES 2.0

5 cups of sliced apples
¾ cup of flour
1 teaspoon of cinnamon
1 cup of brown sugar
¾ cup of rolled oats
½ cup of butter

Arrange apples in a buttered pan. Combine sugar, flour, oats and cinnamon. Cut in butter until crumbly. Press over apples. Bake at 350 degrees for about 45 minutes.

BABY CARROTS ON BOARD

2 pounds of baby carrots
½ cup of brown sugar
½ cup of fresh squeezed orange juice
3 tablespoons of butter
¾ teaspoon of cinnamon
¼ teaspoon of nutmeg
2 tablespoons of cornstarch
¼ cup of water

Combine all but the final 2 ingredients in a slow cooker. Cover and cook on low for 3 to 4 hours. Carrots should be tender but crisp, not mushy. Pour of the juice into a small pan. Put carrots in a baking dish. Bring juice to a boil and add the water and cornstarch mixture. Stir and boil for one minute until thick. Pour sauce over carrots in the baking dish.

BEST LITTLE S'MORES HOUSE
IN TEXAS

¼ cup of popcorn kernels
1 tablespoon of oil
Salt (optional)
2 tablespoons of cocoa powder
¼ cup of powdered sugar
¼ cup of graham crack crumbs
¼ cup of mini-marshmallows

Put oil and popcorn in the bottom of a disposable pie tin. Seal the tin with foil in the shape of a large dome. Think of it as a rustic Jiffy Pop. Grill over high heat until popping stops, about 8 minutes. You can salt here and eat basic popcorn. To turn it into S'mores, toss the warm popcorn in a bowl with remaining ingredients.

BURGERTIME

1 pound of ground beef
8 slices of bacon
1 onion
2 cloves of garlic, crushed
2 teaspoons of grated horseradish
4 slices of American or Cheddar cheese
2 tablespoons of oil
Pepper
4 hamburger buns

Finely dice 1 onion and mix with ground beef. Now add garlic, horseradish and pepper to the meat, mix thoroughly and shape into 4 patties. Wrap each patty in 2 slices of bacon, cover and chill for at least 60 minutes. Cook burgers in a skillet or a broiler for 4 to 5 minutes per side or to desired doneness. Top meat with cheese or cook for final minute with cheese on top of meat.

CABBAGE PATCH SALAD

1 purple cabbage
1 green cabbage
1 cup of cheese
1 red onion, sliced
1 green pepper
Salt, pepper and garlic salt
French dressing

Finely cut cabbages, cheese, bologna onion and pepper. Toss in tomato as an option. Add seasonings to taste. Once these are all tossed together, refrigerate at least 8 hours and serve cold with dressing of choice.

CHERNOBYL CHILI

1 pound of ground beef
½ onion, chopped
1 green pepper, chopped
1 package of chili seasoning
1 large can of small red beans, drained
1 large can of chili beans
1 medium whole can tomatoes, diced
Salt, pepper and cumin to taste
Dave's Insanity Sauce to taste

Brown the ground beef then add chopped onion and green pepper. Drain the grease. Add chili seasoning, red beans, chili beans and tomatoes and stir. When mixture begins to boil, turn the heat to low and cook for 2 hours covered.

CHILDREN OF THE CORNBREAD

1 cup of flour
¼ cup of sugar
2 teaspoons of baking powder
1 teaspoon of baking soda
½ teaspoon of salt
1¼ cups of yellow corn meal
1½ cups of low-fat or regular buttermilk
1 large egg
1 cup sharp cheddar cheese, grated
4 thick slices of cooked bacon, shredded
2 tablespoons unsalted butter, melted
   (plus softened butter for greasing pan)

Sift flour, sugar, baking powder, baking soda and salt into a bowl. Add cornmeal and mix well. Mix buttermilk, egg and butter in a separate bowl. Pour flour mixture over buttermilk mixture and stir slowly until combined. Add bacon and cheese and stir. Pour into a lightly greased 9-inch pan and bake at 400 degrees for about 20 minutes.

COUCH POTATOES

2½ pounds of red potatoes
¼ cup of olive oil
2 teaspoons of salt
¼ teaspoon of paprika
½ teaspoon of pepper

Rinse, dry and chop potatoes into cubes. Combine oil, salt, paprika and pepper. Mix well. Add potatoes and toss. Place on an oiled tray. Bake at 425 degrees for 45 minutes until tender and well browned. Turn every 15 minutes.

CYNDI'S TEA BOP

2 cups of boiling water
1 family size tea bag (or 4 to 6 small bags)
¾ cups of sugar
12 ounce can of frozen lemonade concentrate
2 quarts of water
3 teaspoons of vanilla extract
3 teaspoons of almond extract

Steep tea bag in boiling water for 5 minutes then remove bag. Mix tea with remaining ingredients.

DAN'S QUAIL

6 quail
4 tablespoons of Worcestershire
1 tablespoon of olive oil
1 stick of butter
2 tablespoons of molasses
1 teaspoon of mustard
3 lemons
Salt and pepper
Water

Place quail in a roasting pan and pour in enough water to cover the bottom. Cover and bake at 300 degrees for 30 minutes. Remove from oven. Pour a sauce over the birds made from the remaining ingredients. Return to oven and cook for an additional 35 minutes. Baste often. During the final 10 minutes, remove cover on roasting pan to brown the birds.

DEAD MAN'S PARTY MIX

1 cup of chow mein noodles
1 cup of small pretzels or pieces
1 cup of Rice Chex cereal
1 cup of Wheat Chex cereal
½ cup of pecans
½ cup of salted peanuts
¼ cup of butter, melted
2 tablespoons of soy sauce
1½ teaspoons of Worcestershire sauce
1 teaspoon of seasoned salt
¼ teaspoon of garlic powder
½ teaspoon of onion powder (optional)

Combine melted butter with seasonings, sauces and spices. Stir until well mixed. Combine noodles, nuts, pretzels and cereal in a baking dish. Pour liquid over dry ingredients and stir to coat thoroughly. Bake at 250 degrees for 1 hour. Stir 3 or 4 times during baking.

DIFF'RENT STICKS

1 cup of cornmeal
1 cup of buttermilk
1 egg
3 tablespoons of bacon drippings
2 teaspoons of baking powder
½ teaspoon of baking soda
¾ teaspoon of salt

Sift cornmeal, baking powder, soda and salt into a bowl. Stir in buttermilk, egg and bacon drippings until mixed. Spoon the batter into a heated, well-greased cast iron corn stick pan. Bake at 450 degrees for 20 minutes or until golden brown. Can also be made in a cast iron skillet.

FETTUCCINE ALF-REDO

1 pound of fettuccine or pasta
1 cup of butter
4 ounces of canned mushrooms, sliced
¼ cup of Mozzarella cheese, shredded
½ cup of Parmesan or Romano cheese, grated
½ teaspoon of salt
½ teaspoon of garlic powder
¼ teaspoon of oregano
Pepper

Cook noodles or pasta in boiling water according to package directions and drain. Be careful not to overcook. Melt butter in a skillet and add remaining ingredients except cheeses. Stir and cook for a few minutes. Add Romano cheese to noodles and add into butter mixture. Top with Mozzarella cheese.

GAG ME WITH A SPOON STEW

2 pounds of beef, cubed
3 onions, sliced
6 carrots, sliced
½ pound of mushrooms (fresh or canned)
1 cup of celery, diced
2 cloves of garlic, crushed
1½ cups of canned tomatoes
½ cup of red wine

Place all ingredients in a large casserole dish. Put dish in a cold oven. Turn oven to 250 degrees and bake for 5 hours. Do not stir.

GIRLS JUST WANT TO HAVE NACHOS

2 green onions, diced
½ bag of tortilla chips
1 cup of cheese, shredded
2 ounces of olives, sliced
2 tablespoons of sour cream
1 can of refried beans
Salsa

Pour the chips into a baking dish. Spread refried beans evenly over the chips and sprinkle with grated cheese. Bake mixture at 350 degrees for 10 to 15 minutes or until cheese is melted. When it's time to serve top with salsa, olives green onions and sour cream.

GOONY GORP

Raisins
Dry roasted peanuts or almonds
Sunflower seeds, shelled
Rolled Oats
M&Ms, carob, chocolate or vanilla chips

Mix equal parts of each ingredient and store in a sealed container or plastic bag.

HAULIN' OATS GRANOLA

3 cups of rolled oats
¾ cup of raisins
½ cup of sweetened coconut, shredded
½ cup of almonds, sliced
¼ cup of wheat germ
¼ cup of honey
¼ cup of seeds or nuts of choice (optional)
¼ cup of vegetable oil
2½ tablespoons of water
2 tablespoons of brown sugar
¾ teaspoon of vanilla extract
¼ teaspoon of salt

In bowl #1, mix oats, coconut, almonds, wheat germ and seeds/nuts of choice. In bowl #2, mix honey, oil, water, brown sugar, vanilla and salt. Now pour the wet mixture over the dry mixture and coat thoroughly. Spread the granola mixture on a baking sheet and bake at 350 degrees for 25 minutes. Lightly stir granola every 5 minutes to bake evenly. Mixture is done when it's golden brown. Be careful not to burn.

HEAT OF THE MOMENT ASIA CHICKEN

6 boneless, skinless chicken breast halves
¼ cup of hot chili oil
3 tablespoons of hot chili sauce
2 tablespoons of honey
1 tablespoon of paprika
6 green onions
Salt

Combine oil, chili sauce, honey and paprika in a shallow pan. Mince 1 green onion and add to this sauce. Remove half of this mixture and set aside. In the remaining liquid, marinate the chicken in the refrigerator for 3 hours, turning after 90 minutes. Before cooking, sprinkle chicken with remaining onions and salt. Barbecue the chicken until thoroughly cooked and onions are softened. This should take 12 to 18 minutes. If you prefer to use an oven, bake at 375 degrees for 25 to 30 minutes. When you are done with cooking, drizzle remaining sauce on chicken and serve.

HUSH YUPPIES

1 pound of corn meal
1 egg
1 tablespoon of baking powder
1 tablespoon of sugar
1 cup of buttermilk
Pinch of salt

Mix ingredients together, adding a little water of too dry. Form into balls. Cook in skillet or deep fat fryer at 350 degrees.

JACK & STEAK DIANE

1 pound of beef medallions,
   ½-inch to ¾-inch thick
3 teaspoons of lemon pepper
2 tablespoons of olive oil
8 ounces of mushrooms
2 tablespoons of onion, finely diced
2 tablespoons of brandy
2 tablespoons of Worcestershire sauce
½ cup of whipping cream

Heat 1 tablespoon of olive oil in a large pan. Add mushrooms and onions and cook for 3 minutes or until tender. Remove from skillet and clean out pan. Press lemon pepper into beef. Heat the other tablespoon of oil in the pan. Cook for 4 to 7 minutes depending on rare to medium in doneness. Depending on the size of beef this may be done in 2 batches. Remove beef and add brandy to the pan. Cook and stir for a few minutes. Then add cream and Worcestershire sauce. Pour in mushroom mixture, cook and stir until thickened. Add back the medallions, stir and coat with sauce.

LIKE A VIRGIN DAIQUIRI

1 ounce of lime juice
3 ounces of strawberries
1 tablespoon of sugar
Crushed ice

Put ice in a blender, followed by lime juice, sugar and strawberries. Blend until smooth then pour into a chilled glass.

MALL PRETZELS

3½ cups of flour
1½ cups of warm water
1 tablespoon of yeast
1 tablespoon of sugar
Coarse salt

Mix water, yeast and sugar. Add flour gradually until a dough ball forms. Dough should be workable but not sticky. Don't over knead. Put some oil on your hands so dough won't cling to your hands. Divide dough in half, then in quarters. Make 3 dough balls from each quarter. Roll each ball into a rope then twist into a pretzel. Place on a baking sheet and sprinkle with salt. Bake for 12 to 15 minutes. Top with mustard or pizza sauce.

MARTHA & THE BRAN MUFFINS

1 cup of whole-wheat flour
2 teaspoons of baking soda
1½ cups of wheat bran
½ cup of raisins
½ cup of honey
2 tablespoons of butter, room temperature
2 eggs, beaten
¾ cup of milk

Combine dry ingredients in a bowl. Stir in raisins. In a second bowl, cream butter and honey together until smooth. Add well-beaten eggs and blend. Add milk and continue beating until smooth. In the center of the dry mixture add the batter. Stir gently until dry ingredients are moistened. Don't over mix. Drop mixture into 12 greased muffin tins. Bake at 350 degrees for 20 to 25 minutes.

M*A*S*H BROWN POTATOES

2 pounds of frozen hash browns
2 cups of cheddar cheese, shredded
1 cup of sour cream
1 can of cream of chicken soup
½ cup of butter
½ teaspoon of onion flakes

Melt butter in a pot then add soup, cheese, sour cream and onion flakes. Mix thoroughly. Put hash browns in a 9-inch by 13-inch pan. Pour soup mixture over the hash browns. Bake at 350 degrees for 75 minutes.

MIAMI RICE

5 green onions
½ green pepper, diced
4 stalks of celery
3 tablespoons of margarine or butter
1 cup of raw rice
1 cup of mushrooms (drained if canned)
4 tablespoons of parsley, chopped
2 cups chicken bouillon or stock

Sauté green onions, green pepper and celery in margarine. Stir in rice and add chicken bouillon. Cook covered for 20 to 30 minutes. For the last 10 minutes, add mushrooms and parsley and leave cover off. Put in casserole or baking dish to heat.

MIDNIGHT CHICKEN RUN

3 pounds of chicken parts, skin removed
¼ cup of flour
1 tablespoon of butter, melted
1 teaspoon of paprika
½ teaspoon of crushed red pepper
½ teaspoon of black pepper
¼ teaspoon of salt

Place dry ingredients in a brown paper bag and shake to mix. Coat chicken parts with melted butter and put in bag and shake. Put chicken pieces in a baking pan or dish. Bake at 375 degrees for 45 to 50 minutes.

MIGHTY MORPHIN' CHICKEN WINGS

24 chicken wings
1 cup of pineapple juice
1 cup of soy sauce
1 cup of sugar
¼ cup of water
¼ cup of vegetable oil
2 cloves of garlic, crushed
1 teaspoon of ginger

Combine all ingredients in pan except chicken and ginger. Once thoroughly combined, add ginger and refrigerate overnight. Next day, pour off about 1 cup of liquid and place chicken in the pan. Bake uncovered at 350 degrees for 60 minutes. Baste wings with remaining liquid during baking.

MR. T-BONE STEAK

2 steaks
1 cup of soy sauce
1 cup of sherry
½ cup of peanut oil
3 small garlic cloves, minced
½ teaspoon of ground ginger

Blend soy sauce, sherry, oil, cloves and ginger thoroughly. Pour the mixture into a non-metallic dish or bowl. Place steaks in the liquid and marinate in the refrigerator for at least 6 hours, turning steaks after 3 hours. When ready to grill or fry, cook for 4 to 6 minutes per side.

NEW WAVE CHOWDER

1 pound of haddock or cod fillets,
   cut into small pieces
1½ cups of water
½ cup of milk
1 tablespoon of butter
¾ cup of onion, diced
1 clove of garlic
1 bay leaf
1 sprig of parsley
½ teaspoon of thyme
Fresh ground black pepper

Melt butter in a pan and sauté onions and garlic. Add in remaining ingredients and simmer for 45 minutes.

NOTHING COMPARES 2 ROUX

1 cup of milk
¼ cup of butter
¼ cup of flour
¼ teaspoon of salt
1/8 teaspoon of pepper

Melt butter slowly in a small pan over low heat. Slowly stir in flour, pepper and salt. Continue to heat until the mixture simmers for a minute and is smooth. Stir in milk and continue to heat until mixture boils. Stir for 1 minute while boiling then remove from heat.

PAC MANICOTTI

4 cups of marinara sauce
12 manicotti shells
16 ounces of ricotta cheese
2 egg whites
½ teaspoon of nutmeg
2 tablespoons of basil leaves
¼ teaspoon of black pepper
¾ cup of Parmesan cheese, grated
1½ cups of Mozzarella cheese
10 ounces of frozen spinach,
    chopped, thawed and drained

Cook manicotti shells in unsalted water according to package directions. Mix ricotta cheese, egg whites, nutmeg, basil, pepper, mozzarella, spinach and half of the Parmesan in a large bowl. Pour enough sauce into a 9-inch by 13-inch baking dish to make it about 1-inch deep, about half of the sauce. Stuff the shells with the cheese mixture and arrange in the dish. Pour remaining sauce over the shells, cover the pan with foil and bake at 350 degrees for 25 minutes. Remove foil and sprinkle remaining Parmesan cheese over shells. Bake uncovered for another 10 minutes.

PIE HARD

1 prepared graham cracker piecrust
12 ounces of key lime yogurt
1 small package of lime gelatin
¼ cup of boiling water
8 ounces of whipped topping

In a large bowl, dissolve gelatin in boiling water. Stir in yogurt with a whisk. Fold in whipped topping. Spread into the piecrust and refrigerate overnight.

POUR SOME SUGAR ON ME COOKIES

4½ cups of flour
1 cup of butter, softened
1 cup of vegetable oil
1 cup of sugar
1 cup of powdered sugar, sifted
2 eggs
1 teaspoon of vanilla extract
1 teaspoon of baking soda
1 teaspoon of salt
1 teaspoon of cream of tartar

Combine butter, oil and sugars in a large bowl and beat well. Add eggs one at a time, beating after each one the stir in vanilla. Now combine flour, soda, salt and cream of tartar in a large bowl. Add both mixtures and beat well. Shape dough into 1-inch balls and placed on ungreased cookie sheets. Dip the bottom of a glass in sugar and flatten each dough ball. Bake at 350 degrees for 9 minutes. Remove from oven and let cool on wire rack.

PREPPIE PASTA SALAD

1 package of tri-colored pasta
1 small bottle of Italian dressing
1 package of Italian dressing mix
1 sliced medium cucumber
1 cup of cherry tomatoes
6 ounces of large olives, canned
1 avocado, diced

Cook pasta, drain and rinse in cold water. Add dry dressing, cucumber, tomatoes and avocado to the pasta. Stir in ½ bottle of dressing and add olives.

PRIVATE IDAHO POTATOES

4 russet potatoes cut into 1-inch chunks
2 teaspoons of olive oil
3 cloves of garlic, minced
1 teaspoon of rosemary
1 teaspoon or oregano
¼ teaspoon of black pepper
½ teaspoon of salt

Spray a cookie sheet with nonstick spray. In a bowl combine the potato chunks with all ingredients. Thoroughly coat the potatoes. Spread the potatoes on the sheet and bake at 375 degrees for about 35 minutes or until browned. Turn the potatoes a few times.

PUMPKINHEAD SOUP

1 stick of butter
1 onion coarsely chopped
5 pounds of pumpkin
1 cup of heavy cream
1 quart of water
1 pinch of nutmeg
Salt and pepper

Wash and peel pumpkin and remove seeds. Cut pumpkin into 2-inch cubes. Melt butter in large pot and add onions. Cook onions until tender. Add pumpkin and water. Season with salt, pepper and nutmeg. Simmer for 20 to 30 minutes. Puree mixture and add cream. If too thick add water.

PUNCH OUT

2 cups of lime juice
4 cups of sugar
6 cups of rum
8 cups of cold water with ice

Mix ingredients thoroughly until sugar is dissolved.
Serve cold over ice.

RAIDERS OF THE LOST PORK

3 pound boneless pork roast
3 tablespoons of dried cranberries
3 tablespoons of red onion, diced
2 tablespoons of plum sauce
¼ cup of jellied cranberry sauce
Garlic salt
Pepper
Rosemary

Poke a hole in the roast. Stuff the hole with dried cranberries and onion. Mix garlic salt, pepper and rosemary together and rub on the roast. Place in a baking dish and bake at 350 degrees for 45 minutes. In a small pan, warm the cranberry jelly and plum sauce. Pour this mixture over the pork and bake for an additional 20 minutes.

ROASTBUSTERS

4 pound beef roast
1 can of mushroom soup
1 package of dry onion soup mix
2 tablespoons of A-1 steak sauce

Brush the roast with A-1 steak sauce. Sprinkle the dry onion soup on the meat. Set the roast on a piece of aluminum foil in a pan. Pour the soup over the meat and wrap the roast in the foil. Bake at 350 degrees for 2½ hours.

ROBOCHOP

4 pork chops
16 ounces of stewed tomatoes
1 onion, diced
1 green bell pepper, sliced
1 tablespoon of Worcestershire sauce
2 teaspoons of parsley flakes
1 teaspoon of salt
½ teaspoon of pepper
Garlic powder to taste
Dash or two of hot sauce

In a skillet, brown chops on both sides over medium heat. Add in remaining ingredients, stir and reduce the heat. Cover and simmer for 30 or until everything is done.

ROCK THE CASH BAR PUNCH

20 cups of ginger ale
12 cups of orange juice
10 cups of sugar
10 cups of water
6 cups of pineapple juice
8 cups of lemon juice
8 cups of grape juice
Alcohol of choice

Mix liquids and thoroughly dissolve sugar. Spike with a fifth of your favorite vodka, rum or bourbon, two fifths if you're feeling dangerous and want to trash a hotel room.

ROMANCING THE BONES

2 packages of country style ribs
¾ cup of brown sugar
¾ cup of vinegar
2 tablespoons of cornstarch
1 cup of pineapple bits
½ cup of ketchup
½ cup of water
¼ cup of chopped onion
2 tablespoons of soy sauce
2 teaspoons of dry mustard

Bake the ribs at 450 degrees for 30 minutes in a pan or dish. Mix all ingredients thoroughly in a pan and heat until it is thick and boiling. Pour the sauce over the fibs and bake at 325 degrees for 2 hours. Baste the meat occasionally.

SKINNY TIE PASTA

2 cans of chicken broth
1/3 pound of shrimp, fresh and cleaned
12 mushrooms chopped into quarters
1 green onion, sliced
Angel hair pasta

Bring chicken broth to a boil the drop mushrooms in. Gently boil for 5 minutes. Add in the cleaned shrimp and boil for 3 minutes. Add in green onion and boil for another minute. Strain ingredients and add them into the pasta and toss. Pour broth over everything for desired flavor.

ST. ELMO'S CAMPFIRE BURGERS

1 pound of hamburger
1 onion
2 carrots
2 potatoes
Salt and pepper to taste
4 hamburger buns

Make burger patties and place on aluminum foil. Thinly slice onions, carrots and potatoes and place on top of meat. Salt and pepper to taste. Fold foil into a pocket and fold edges over. Cook over the campfire.

SUNDAY BLOODY MARY SUNDAY

3 ounces of tomato juice
1½ ounces of vodka
½ ounce of lemon juice
4 drops of Worcestershire sauce
Celery salt
Ground pepper
Hot pepper to taste
Celery stalk
Ice

Pour liquid ingredients into a shaker and shake well then pour over ice in a tall glass. Add seasonings to taste and garnish with a celery stalk.

THE BIG CHILLED SHRIMP DIP

4 ounces of shrimp
½ cup of celery, chopped
½ cup of onion, diced
½ cup of mayonnaise
1 small package of cream cheese
1½ teaspoons of lemon juice

Chop shrimp into pieces. Mix with additional ingredients and chill for 3 hours in the refrigerator.

THE BOYS OF SUMMER SALAD

1 cup of pineapple bits
1 cup of mandarin oranges
1 cup of mini marshmallows
1 cup of shredded coconut
1 cup of sour cream

Mix ingredients thoroughly and refrigerate for 4 hours then serve.

THE BREAKFAST OMELET CLUB

18 eggs
2 cups of shredded cheddar cheese
1 cup of fresh mushrooms, sliced
1 cup of sour cream
1 cup of milk
½ cup of butter
½ cup of green onions, diced
2 teaspoons of salt
¼ teaspoon of basil

Place butter in a baking dish and melt in the oven. Beat eggs with milk, sour cream, salt and basil. Stir in remaining ingredients and pour into the baking dish. Bake at 325 degrees, uncovered for 40 to 45 minutes.

THE MIRACLE ON RICE

1 cup of wild rice, thoroughly rinsed
1 cup of chicken soup
3 cups of water
¼ cup of celery
¼ cup of onions
¼ cup of mushrooms
2 tablespoons of almond slivers (optional)
2 tablespoons of margarine or butter

Cook rice in water for 45 to 55 minutes in a covered pot. Sauté remaining ingredients together in a separate pan. When rice is tender add in the sautéed ingredients and stir.

THE MONEY PIT BARBECUE
(This recipe can cook up to 300 pounds of meat)

5 pounds of Morton sugar-cure salt
5 pounds of brown sugar
7 pounds of salt
8 ounces of pepper
2 ounces of garlic salt
2 ounces of celery salt
1¾ ounces of paprika
1 ounce of cayenne pepper

Mix ingredients thoroughly. Prepare your meat in 5 and 10 pound chunks. Roll each piece of meat in the mixture. Place 10 pounds of meat in a wet flour sack, then put the flour sack in a wet burlap sack. In a deep pit, burn wood all day to make a bed of coals. Put a layer of large rocks on the coals and put wet sack of meat on the rocks. Cover the pit with metal lids or sheet metal and pile 12 to 15 inches of dirt on the metal. Leave alone for 24 hours. Remove dirt carefully, lift out sacks, cut open and serve.

THE TERMINATOR CHILI

6 pounds of beef, cubed
3 onions, diced
7 cloves of garlic, minced
3 bottles of beer
¼ cup of tomato paste
3 tablespoons of chili peppers, ground
2 tablespoons of oregano
2 tablespoons of coriander, ground
2 tablespoons of salt
1 tablespoon of lemon juice
1 tablespoon of hot mustard
1 tablespoon of sugar
1 tablespoon of marjoram
1 tablespoon of paprika
2 teaspoons of cayenne pepper
2 teaspoons of Worcestershire sauce
2 teaspoons of Frank's Red Hot sauce
1 teaspoon of Tabasco sauce
1 teaspoon of cinnamon
¼ teaspoon of cumin seed
Bacon grease

In a pot, brown beef and onions in bacon grease. Drain grease, add beer and simmer for 15 minutes. Add remaining ingredients and mix. Simmer 2 to 4 hours or until beef is tender, stir occasionally.

THE WOK-MAN

3 to 4 chicken breasts, boneless and skinless
2 cups of water
2 teaspoons of salt
2 teaspoons of soda
4 tablespoons of oil
Teriyaki sauce
Celery, diced
Onion, diced
Carrots, sliced
Mushrooms, sliced

Wash and soak chicken breasts in water with salt and soda for 30 minutes. Rinse the meat and dice into small pieces. Place pieces in a covered dish with teriyaki sauce and marinate for 3 hours. Remove from the marinade and dry with paper towels. In a wok, fry quickly in 2 tablespoons of oil the remove. Clean the pan and fry the vegetables in 2 tablespoons of oil. When done stir in the diced chicken to warm. Serve over rice or noodles.

TURNED-UP COLLAR GREENS

1 large bunch of collard greens
  (kale or chard can be used)
1 tablespoon of olive oil
3 cloves or garlic, minced
Juice from ½ a lemon
Salt and pepper to taste

Use the top portion of the greens and wash thoroughly. Cut leaves into strips and stack leaves on top of each other in a bowl. Heat oil in a skillet and sauté garlic for a few minutes until golden brown. Add greens to the pan and stir to coat. Stir frequently until the greens are tender. Depending on the greens it could take 3 to 8 minutes. Remove from heat and add lemon juice and vinegar. Salt and pepper to taste.

WHAT I LIKE ABOUT EWE

6 lamb chops
1 green pepper, sliced
1 onion, sliced
1 lemon, sliced
2 cups of tomato juice
Oil

Brown the chops in a little bit of oil in a pan. Place the meat in a baking dish. Top each chop with a slice of green pepper, an onion ring and a lemon slice. Carefully pour tomato juice over the chops. Cover the dish and bake at 325 degrees for 90 minutes.

WHO COOKED ROGER RABBIT?

2 rabbits cut into pieces
2 tablespoons of butter or shortening
2 cans of cream of mushroom soup

Melt butter and shortening in a large skillet. Place rabbit pieces in skillet to brown, cooking only to half way. Now put rabbit in a baking dish and cover with cream of mushroom soup. Cover with foil and bake at 350 degrees for 45 minutes.

A FISH CALLED TUNA

1 can of tuna, drained and flake
1 can of cream of celery soup
¼ cup of milk
2 hard-boiled eggs, diced
1 cup of cooked peas
½ cup of crumbled potato chips

In a greased baking dish, blend soup and milk. Stir in tuna, eggs and peas. Top with potato chip crumbs. Bake at 350 degrees for 25 minutes

A FLOCK OF SEA BASS

10 to 12 ounces sea bass fillets (4), cleaned
½ cup of parsley leaves, loosely packed
¼ cup of white wine vinegar or white wine
3 cloves of garlic, crushed
2 tablespoons of pepper, coarsely ground
1 tablespoon of olive oil
2 teaspoons of kosher salt

Mix garlic, oil salt and pepper thoroughly. Place fillets in a glass or ceramic baking dish. Rub the mixture over the fish then pour wine/vinegar over the fish. Bake fish at 450 degrees for 15 minutes. Sprinkle with parsley and bake for 3 more minutes. When fish looks opaque and flakes easily it is done.

ALLIGATOR DUNDEE STEW

3 pounds of diced alligator meat
½ cup of oil
2 cups of diced onions
1 cup of diced celery
1 cup of diced bell pepper
2 tablespoons of chopped garlic
2 tablespoons of diced jalapenos
16 ounces of pinto beans (canned)
24 ounces of tomato sauce
1 cup of chicken stock
1 tablespoon of chili powder
1 tablespoon of cumin
Salt and pepper

In a large pot or Dutch oven, heat oil over medium to high heat. Add gator meat and cook for 20 minutes. Add in onions, celery, bell pepper, garlic and jalapenos and sauté until vegetables are wilted, about 3 to 5 minutes. Add in pinto beans, tomato sauce and chicken stock. Bring to a boil and reduce to a simmer. Add chili powder and cumin and stir well. Cook for one hour. Stir occasionally. Once the meat is tender season to taste with salt and pepper.

ANOTHER ONE BITES THE CRUST

1 package of refrigerated crescent rolls
1 pound of pork sausage, fried and crumbled
1 cup of hash brown potatoes, thawed
1 cup of Cheddar cheese, shredded
2 tablespoons of Parmesan cheese, grated
¼ cup of milk
½ teaspoon of salt
5 eggs
Pepper to taste

Press rolls into a 12-inch pizza pan to form the crust. Layer with potatoes and then Cheddar cheese. Beat eggs and blend with milk, salt and pepper. Mix thoroughly and pour onto crust. Sprinkle with Parmesan cheese. Bake at 375 degrees for 25 to 30 minutes.

B.A.K.E. IN THE U.S.A.

3 eggs, slightly beaten
1 cup of light or dark corn syrup
1 cup of sugar
4 tablespoons of melted butter
1 teaspoon of vanilla
1½ cups of pecan halves
1 9-inch pie shell, unbaked

In a bowl mix eggs, syrup, sugar, butter and vanilla until well blended. Stir in pecan halves then pour into pie shell. Bake at 350 degrees for 50 to 55 minutes. Test for doneness with a knife. Insert it into the center and if it comes out clean, it's ready.

BANANA RAMA SQUARES

2 cups of quick-cooking rolled oats
¾ cup of mashed banana
½ cup of brown sugar, packed
1 egg
6 tablespoons of butter
¼ teaspoon of salt
¼ cup of walnuts, chopped (optional)

Mix butter and sugar together until smooth. Add egg to the mixture and beat thoroughly. Mix in salt and mashed banana and blend until smooth. Finally, stir in oats and optional walnuts. Spread mixture into a lightly greased 8-inch by 8-inch pan or baking dish. Bake at 350 for 55 minutes or until firm. Let cool and slice.

BEAT IT BREAD

5 large ripe bananas
4 eggs
4 cups of flour
2 cups of sugar
1 cup of oil
2 teaspoons of baking soda

Beat and mash the bananas into a liquid. Then beat the eggs until fluffy. Combine bananas and eggs then stir in sugar and oil and beat the mixture. Add in flour and baking soda and beat it until smooth. Pour mixture into 2 greased loaf pans. Bake at 350 degrees for 40 to 50 minutes.

BILLY OCEAN PERCH

2 pounds of ocean perch fillets (6 to 8)
2 cups of corn flakes, crushed
1 egg, lightly beaten
1 tablespoon of parsley, dried
Old Bay seasoning
Garlic powder

Mix corn flakes with Old Bay, parsley and garlic powder to taste. Dip fish in egg then dip top of fish in corn flakes. Spray a baking pan or dish with cooking spray or lightly grease. Put fish in the dish and bake at 350 degrees for 20 to 25 minutes or until fish flakes easily.

BIRD UP

6 chicken breasts, skinless and boneless
2 cups of mushroom soup
2 cups of cream of chicken soup
1 cup of bourbon
1 cup of water chestnuts, sliced
1 cup of mushrooms

Put chicken breasts in a baking dish. Mix remaining ingredients together and pour over chicken. Bake at 325 degrees for 90 minutes to 2 hours.

BLACK ICED COFFEE N BED

6 cups of hot coffee
10 cloves, whole
10 allspice, whole
¼ cup of sugar
2 cinnamon sticks
2 black peppercorns

Combine coffee, sugar, cloves, allspice peppercorns and cinnamon sticks and stir well. Let stand at room temperature for 1 hour. Strain and serve over ice.

BLONDIES

1 cup of brown sugar
¾ cup flour, sifted
½ cup of nuts, chopped (optional)
1 egg
¼ cup of butter
1 teaspoon of vanilla
1 teaspoon of baking powder
½ teaspoon of salt

In a pan, melt the butter slowly. Remove the butter from the heat and stir in brown sugar. Let the mixture cool and beat in the egg. Mix the dry ingredients together. Combine the brown sugar mixture wit the dry ingredients then add the vanilla and mix thoroughly. Spread the batter in a lightly-greased 8-inch by 8-inch pan. Bake at 350 degrees for 30 to 35 minutes. Let cool and cut into squares.

BUST A MOO

3 pounds of beef short ribs,
   cut into bite-sized pieces
1 onion, diced
1 cup of ketchup
½ cup of celery, diced
½ cup of water
¼ cup of vinegar
3 tablespoons of Worcestershire sauce
2 tablespoons of sugar
2 tablespoons of shortening
2 teaspoons
1 teaspoon of mustard

Melt shortening in a big skillet. Brown the meat in the skillet with the diced onion. Add in the remaining ingredients. Cover the pan and bake at 350 degrees for 2 hours.

CARMEL CHAMELEONS

2 cups of brown sugar, firmly packed
1 cup of flour
2 eggs
2/3 cup of oil or melted shortening
2 teaspoons of vanilla
2 teaspoons of baking powder
½ teaspoon of salt
1 cup of chopped nuts (optional)

In a bowl combine melted butter, shortening, brown sugar vanilla, unbeaten eggs, nuts (optional). Then add sifted dry ingredients in this order: flour, baking powder and salt. Mix thoroughly and spread evenly on a baking pan or jellyroll pan. Bake at 350 degrees for 25. Be careful NOT to over bake these caramel brownies. Test with a toothpick in the last 5 minutes. You want them chewy and not dry.

CHERRY BOMB PORK CHOPS

4 pork chops, ½-inch thick
1 tablespoon of shortening
1 tablespoon of cider vinegar
16 ounces of pitted light cherries w/syrup
¼ cup of slivered almonds
6 whole cloves
Salt and pepper to taste

Brown pork chops in a skillet with shortening, season with salt and pepper. Mix cherries and syrup with almonds, cloves and vinegar. Drain shortening and pour cherry mixture over the chops. Simmer for 30 minutes.

CHOCOLATE C.H.I.P.S

12 ounces of chocolate chips
3 cups of whole-wheat flour
1 cup of sugar
1 cup of brown sugar
2/3 cup of shortening
2/3 cup of butter, softened
2 eggs
2 teaspoons of vanilla
1 teaspoon of baking soda
1 teaspoon of salt

Mix shortening, butter, sugars, eggs and vanilla together. Stir in wheat flour, baking soda and salt to the mixture. Finally, stir in chocolate chip cookies. Drop spoonfuls on a lightly greased cookie sheet. Bake at 375 degrees for 8 to 10 minutes or until lightly browned.

DIP TO BE SQUARE

8 ounces of softened cream cheese
¼ cup of butterscotch ice cream topping
1 tablespoon of brown sugar
1 teaspoon of vanilla

Combine all ingredients thoroughly in a bowl. Serve with your favorite fruit.

FER SHERBET

½ gallon of pineapple sherbet
1 package of raspberries, frozen
2 bananas

Soften the sherbet and whip in the raspberries. Once thoroughly combined mash bananas and stir in to the mixture.

FINE YOUNG CASSEROLE

4 potatoes, peeled and sliced
1 pound of ground beef
1 onion, sliced thin
10ounce can of tomato soup, undiluted
15 ounces of kidney beans, canned & drained
1 teaspoon of salt
¼ teaspoon of pepper

Grease a baking or casserole dish. Place sliced potatoes on the bottom of the dish. Crumble ground beef over potatoes and sprinkle with pepper and ½ teaspoon of the salt. Spread onions over the meat then layer the beans. Pour tomato soup over everything and sprinkle with remaining ½ teaspoon of salt. Put cover on the dish. Bake at 375 degrees for 30 minutes. Remove cover and continue to bake for 1 more hour.

GREAT WHITE NORTH HOSER STEW EH?

2 pounds of elk or moose in cubes
20 ounces of tomatoes (canned or fresh)
1 box of frozen peas
6 sliced carrots
3 small chopped onions
1 cup of diced celery
3 medium potatoes diced
2 tablespoons of sugar
1 tablespoon of salt
¼ teaspoon of pepper
5 ounces chestnuts, sliced and drained
¼ cup of red wine

Combine all ingredients thoroughly in a baking dish and cover. Bake at 275 degrees for 5 hours.

HOWARD THE ROASTED DUCK

1 duck
¼ unpeeled apple
¼ peeled onion
1 strip of bacon
Salt

Rinse duck well and sprinkle inside with salt. Place the apple and onion inside the duck. Place the bacon over the duck. Put duck in a roasting pan and cover with foil. Bake in an over at 350 degrees for 2 hours. Reduce to 325 degrees for 2 more hours. If needed, add a little water in the pan to keep bird moist during cooking. If duck is not browning enough, remove foil during the last 30 minutes of cooking.

IF I COULD TURN BACK THYME

4 pork chops
2 ounces of mushrooms, sliced
1 can of cream of celery soup
1 cup of carrots, sliced
½ cup of water
¼ teaspoon of thyme, crushed
6 small white onions, whole
Shortening or oil

In a skillet, brown pork chops and mushrooms in shortening or oil. Pour off the liquid, stir in soup, water and thyme. Add onions and carrots. Cook over low heat for 45 minutes or until meat is tender.

JERRY WILD RICE

2 cups of wild rice, cooked
2 eggs, beaten
½ stick of butter
1 pound of cooked shrimp, small pieces
½ cup of water chestnuts, diced
1 tablespoon of soy sauce
2 green onions, chopped (optional)

Melt butter in a skillet the add rice, shrimp and water chestnuts. Cook and stir until thoroughly heated. Mix eggs and soy sauce and combine with rice mixture. Stir quickly until eggs set. Put on a platter and top with green onions.

JESSIE'S GRILL

4 pork chops, 1-inch thick
¼ teaspoon of salt
¾ teaspoon of lemon pepper
½ teaspoon of whole, dried oregano leaves

Mix salt, lemon pepper and oregano and coat the pork chops. Grill over low to medium heat for 25 minutes or until chops are no longer pink. Turn them once.

LARRY BARBECUED BIRD

3 pounds of chicken
3 tablespoons of honey
3 tablespoons of mustard
1 tablespoon of sesame seeds

Barbecue chicken on the grill or bake in the oven.
Mix honey, mustard and sesame seeds. Ten minutes
before taking off the heat, brush the chicken with
the mixture.

LET MY FUDGE OPEN THE DOOR

¾ cup of powdered milk
½ cup of peanut butter
¼ cup of honey

Mix together thoroughly and smooth into an 8-inch by 8-inch pan. Chill overnight.

LIKE TOTALLY TOAST

2 cups of milk
4 eggs
½ teaspoon salt
2 teaspoons of cinnamon
Sliced bread
Oil

Beat four eggs thoroughly then mix all of the ingredients together. Dip bread slices into the mixture until well coated. Fry on an oiled griddle or skillet until golden brown.

LISA LISA & CULT HAM

1 pound of ground pork
1 pound of ground ham
1 cup of dry bread crumbs
1 cup of milk
1 egg
1/3 cup of brown sugar
¼ cup of diluted vinegar
1 teaspoon of dry mustard

Mix the pork, ham, breadcrumbs, milk and egg. Put the loaf in a greased loaf pan or baking dish. Bake at 350 degrees for 1 hour. Make a sauce by combining brown sugar, mustard and diluted vinegar. Baste the loaf with this liquid while it cooks.

MILLI VANILLA MILKSHAKE

5 scoops of vanilla ice cream
1 cup of milk (whole or 2%)
1 teaspoon of vanilla extract

Put all ingredients in a blender and blend until smooth.

MONEY FOR DUMPLING

1 cup of sifted flour
1½ teaspoons of baking powder
½ teaspoon of salt
1 egg, well beaten
½ cup of milk
1 teaspoon of melted butter

Sift together dry ingredients. Combine egg, milk and butter. Add liquid gradually to the dry ingredients. Stir until dough is smooth and no longer sticks to the spoon. Divide dough into 12 pieces and drop into a pot of boiling water (or soup). Cover pot and continue to boil for 12 to 15 minutes.

PRIVATE FRIES

6 potatoes, grated
½ cup of milk
1 cup of flour
2 teaspoons of salt
2 eggs
Shortening, oil or lard

Grate potatoes medium fine. Combine with salt, milk eggs and flour. In a skillet, place spoonfuls of the mixture into hot shortening or oil and flatten. Brown both sides of the potato batter.

PULLING MUSSELS FROM THE SHELL

4 dozen mussels, well scrubbed
1 cup of white wine
2 scallions, diced
½ teaspoon of thyme
4 dried bay leaves

Place everything in a large pot over high heat. Bring to a boil. Cover and steam for 20 minutes. If there doesn't seem to me enough liquid, add a little more wine.

RED, RED WINE WITH BEEF

2 pounds of stew beef
1 can of cream of mushroom soup
1 can of cream of celery soup
1 package of dry onion soup mix
1 cup of red cooking wine

Combine all ingredients in a baking dish and mix thoroughly. Cover and cook at 350 degrees for 3 to 3½ hours. Serve over rice or noodles.

ROSEANNE BAR CHEESE

2 pounds of Velveeta cheese
6 ounces of horseradish
8 drops of Tabasco sauce
1 cup of mayonnaise

Combine cheese, Tabasco sauce and horseradish in a double boiler. If you don't have a double boiler, put ingredients in a small pot and place in a larger pot half-filled with water. Once melted, remove from heat and add mayonnaise. Mix thoroughly. Pour into a container and let cool.

SHE-RA PRINCESS OF FLOUR

3½ cups of flour
3 cups of sugar
2 cups of pumpkin, mashed or diced fine
4 eggs
1 cup of oil
2/3 cup of water
2 teaspoons of baking soda
1½ teaspoons of salt
1 teaspoon of nutmeg
1 teaspoon of cinnamon

Mix all of the ingredients thoroughly. Pour the batter into a greased loaf pan and bake at 350 degrees for 1 hour.

STRAY BRAT STRUT

6 brats, cut into quarters
¼ cup of light cream
2 tablespoons of mustard
1 teaspoon of minced onion
¼ teaspoon of pepper
16 ounces of sauerkraut, drained
Hot sauce to taste (optional)
Pinch of paprika
4 sticks or skewers

Put brat pieces on 4 skewers. Make a sauce of the cream, mustard, onion, pepper, paprika and hot sauce. Heat the brats in the oven at 375 degrees for 8 to 12 minutes on foil or a cookie sheet. If you prefer, grill them over medium heat for 8 to 10 minutes. Turn and baste with liquid often. After you've heated the sauerkraut, place meat skewers on a bed of the kraut and pour sauce over it all.

TASTES GREAT LESS FILLING BREAD

3 cups of self-rising flour
3 tablespoons of sugar
3 tablespoons of butter
1 can of beer (12 ounces)

Mix flour, sugar and beer together and place in a greased loaf pan. Bake at 350 degrees for one hour. Split top with a knife and pour on melted butter.

THE BREWS BROTHERS ROOT BEER

2 cups of sugar
½ bottle root beer extract
1 teaspoon of dry yeast
½ cup of warm water
1 to 2 cups water

Pour 3 tablespoons of root beer extract over 2 cups sugar and add just enough water to dissolve. Add 1 of teaspoon dry yeast to ½-cup warm water to dissolve. Add both mixtures together and pour into gallon jug. Top off jug with warm water and let sit for 6 hours uncapped. Tighten lid and refrigerate. After 24 hours it's ready to drink. The longer it sits, the better it tastes.

THE LAST TEMPTATION OF RICE

1 cup of wild rice
1 cup of chicken soup
3 cups water
¼ cup celery
¼ cup onions
¼ cup mushrooms
2 tablespoons almond slivers
2 tablespoons margarine

Cook rice in water for 45 to 55 minutes in a covered pot. Sauté remaining ingredients together in a separate pan. When rice is tender add in the sautéed ingredients and stir.

THE MEATBALL RUN

1 pound of ground chuck
2 cooked potatoes, grated
1 small onion, grated
½ cup of breadcrumbs
¼ of milk
1 egg
½ teaspoon of sugar
Salt and pepper to taste
Butter

Mix all ingredients thoroughly except the butter. Form into 1-inch balls and fry in butter in a skillet.

THE WRATH OF FLAN

2 quarts of milk
4 egg yolks
1 pound of sugar
2 teaspoons of vanilla

Mix sugar, milk and vanilla. Put in a pan and boil for 3 minutes. Remove and cool. Beat eggs with a little milk and add slowly to the cooled mixture. Return to heat and stir continuously until it thickens. Remove from heat and pour into cups. Pour sugar, white or brown, into the skillet. Stir over low heat until sugar melts and is caramelized. Pour over the custard when cool.

TOM'S CRUISIN' COCKTAIL SAUCE

¾ cup of chili sauce
4 tablespoons of lemon juice
1 tablespoon of horseradish
1 teaspoon of Worcestershire sauce
1 teaspoon of onion, finely diced
¼ teaspoon of salt
Pepper to taste

Combine all ingredients thoroughly. Chill in the refrigerator for at least 4 hours.

UNION OF THE STEAK

2 pounds of sirloin steak
16 ounces of seasoned breadcrumbs
½ cup of flour
2 eggs
1 cup of milk
½ cup of oil
1 teaspoon of onion powder
1 teaspoon of garlic powder
¼ teaspoon of salt
Pepper to taste

Flatten steak with a meat hammer to ½-inch thick. Cut into pieces. Mix eggs, milk, onion powder, garlic powder, salt and pepper in a bowl. Fill a second bowl with breadcrumbs. Put flour in a paper of plastic bag. Place meat in the bag and shake to coat. Drop each piece in the egg wash finishing with a roll in the breadcrumbs. Heat oil in the skillet on medium-high heat. Cook steaks for 2 to 3 minutes per side until reaching desired doneness.

VALLEY GIRL SALAD

1 package of tri-colored pasta
1 small bottle of Italian dressing
1 package of Italian dressing mix
1 medium cucumber, sliced
1 cup of cherry tomatoes
6 ounces of olives
1 avocado, diced

Cook pasta, drain and rinse in cold water. Add dry dressing, cucumber, tomatoes and avocado to the pasta. Stir in ½ bottle of dressing and add olives.

VEGEMITE SANDWICH

1 jar of Vegemite
2 slices of whole grain or wheat bread
Butter

Butter one side of each slice of bread. Spread on the Vegemite to the desired thickness. Close of the sandwich and enjoy.

Vegemite is a dark brown food paste made from leftover brewers' yeast extract. Spices and vegetables are added to complete the sandwich spread. It is to Australia what peanut butter is to the USA. It was made famous in the song "Down Under" by Mean At Work

WAKE ME UP BEFORE YOU COCOA

2 cups of zucchini, peeled and shredded
3 eggs
1 cup of oil
2 tablespoons of vanilla
2 cups of flour
1 teaspoon of salt
1½ teaspoons of baking powder
½ cup of cocoa
1 cup of chopped walnuts

Mix wet ingredients in one bowl and dry ingredients in a second bowl. Combine the bowls and add nuts. Grease and flour 2 bread pans. Bake at 350 degrees for 45 to 50 minutes.

WE GOT THE MEAT

1 pound of ground beef
1 cup of cornflakes, crushed
1 green pepper, diced
1 envelope of dry onion soup mix
1 cup of whole kernel corn
2 eggs, beaten
¾ cup of water
¼ cup of ketchup

In a bowl combine all ingredients and mix thoroughly. Put mixture in a loaf pan. Bake at 350 degrees for 1 hour or until completely cooked.

WHERE'S THE BEEF?

1 pound of ground beef
½ onion, diced fine
½ cup of ketchup
1 can of chicken gumbo soup
1 tablespoon of chili powder
6 hamburger buns

In a skillet, brown the ground with the diced onion. Stir the meat while it browns. Add soup and ketchup to the skillet and stir well. Stir in the chili powder and mix thoroughly. Cook for 20 minutes over medium to high heat. Stir occasionally. Serve on the buns.

WHO'S FRYING NOW

1½ cups of scalded milk
1½ cups of wheat flour
2½ cups of white flour
3 tablespoons of butter
3 tablespoons of sugar
1 heaping tablespoon of yeast
¾ teaspoon of salt
1/3 cup of warm water

Add warm water to yeast. Mix all ingredients together. Roll out dough in circles. Make holes in the dough with a fork. Fry in a pan until brown.

WIND BENEATH ME CHICKEN WINGS

20 chicken wings, cut in half
1 cup of soy sauce
1 cup of orange marmalade
4 cloves of garlic, crushed
1 teaspoon of black pepper
1 teaspoon of ginger

Mix soy sauce, marmalade, garlic, pepper and ginger together thoroughly. Place wings in a shallow baking dish or pan. Pour marinade over the chicken, cover the pan and refrigerate for at least 8 hours. Bake the wings uncovered in the sauce at 300 degrees for 45 minutes.

For information on Tim Murphy's entire series
of cookbooks visit www.flanneljohn.com.

Made in the USA
Monee, IL
22 September 2021